MANGO

Ratna M. Dupont

MANGO

(Children's Learning and Character Building Series)

© 2014

Written by Ratna M. DuPont

Illustrated by Charles Berton

Published by Beyond Fear Books

All Rights Reserved.

No parts of this book may be reproduced, digitally or otherwise, without prior written permission from the author.

ISBN-13: 978-0692334874

ISBN-10: 0692334874

Visit Ratna at www.BeyondFearBooks.com

Search "Ratna M. DuPont" on Facebook & like us.

Visit Charles Berton at CharlesBerton.com

This book belongs to:

_____

Acknowledgment

To all the children in my life
who have given me the greatest gift
I could ever ask for:
"Pure Love"

Mango is not a juicy yellow fruit. Mango is a cute little brown and white puppy. Mango belongs to the Jones' family who live in a two-story house on "M" street. The three children in the Jones' family lavish Mango with love.

Mango has a wicker bed and a floppy orange cushion to sleep on. Every morning, Mother Jones puts Mango's wicker bed in a cozy corner where the fresh breeze makes it nice and comfortable for her to take a nap.

When the family is busy, Mango follows little Lisa Jones around the house. Little Lisa will be five years old in August.

When the sun is out and it begins to get hot, Mango and Lisa sit in a shade of the big avocado tree in the backyard. In the cool shade under the big tree, Lisa likes to read Mango children stories. In every story she reads, she makes a special effort to show Mango the colorful pictures on every page.

During the late summer and the early fall, Lisa and Mango spend almost every afternoon under the avocado tree with large avocados precariously hanging over their heads. But, they do not seem to mind, because no avocado has ever fallen on them.

One afternoon, Mrs. Jones appears worried, Lisa has a fever, a runny nose and puffy eyes.

Looking at Mango with sad eyes, Lisa says, "Mango, I would like to go outside and play with you but my mother wants me to stay in bed. Today, you'll have to play by yourself." Mango does not want to play alone. She sits dejected with her head down, and tail between her legs.

Suddenly, she hears a strange sound coming from the backyard and cautiously slips out the back door to investigate.

High in the avocado tree, Mango spots a strange creature sitting on a thick branch.

"Hey, who are you and what are you doing in my avocado tree?" she asks.

With a crazy smile, the strange creature replies, "I'm a cat, you silly pup."

With eyes big as saucers, Mango stares at the cat and mumbles, "You don't look like a cat."

"What do you think I look like? The cat

replies, with a slight hiss.

"I'm not sure, Mango responds. "I've never seen a cat with a sharp pointed face and a brown and tan coat. I think you look like a weasel."

Puffed up with importance, the cat snaps back, "I'm not a weasel, you silly pup! I'm a Siamese cat - a royal Siamese cat."

Wide eyed, Mango chuckles, "I didn't know there are different kinds of cats, because all cats look the same to me."

"I think all dogs look the same. How's that!" The royal Siamese cat replies, with a big toothy grin.

"I guess, like cats, in some ways dogs do look alike. But, I'm not quite certain what those ways are?" Mango replies.

"Hey pup, my first question is, how many dogs have you seen in your short life?"

Sadly, Mango has only seen two dogs, a Chihuahua and a Dachshund.

"Well, my friend, I'm waiting for your answer. Did the cat get your tongue?" The

Siamese quips, laughing out loud.

"I must admit sir, I've seen only two dogs, a Chihuahua who barked at me like a fool, and a Dachshund who tried to roll me over on my back."

"Then, as we say in Siam - as far as dogs go - you are wet behind the ears."

Puzzled, Mango looks up at the cat. "Sir, may I ask how many cats you've seen?"

"My friend, I have seen thousands of cats. Cats in every color of the rainbow, in fact, so many cats, I can't count them all. Poor cats, fat cats, skinny cats, scaredy cats; cats with no bed and cats with plush beds. Luxury cats like my friends Emma and Lou, who live on the 22nd floor of a tall apartment building in New York City. And, homeless cats, in old abandon houses and cars.

"But of all the cats that I have seen, the Persian cat, with its refined Manchu look is the most curious cat of them all."

"Mr. Cat, I do not have much of an education, so please tell me what you mean when you say, Manchu?"

"Manchu have long beards and bushy eyebrows and a very stern look. Their heritage comes from the Mongol invaders who flooded China during the time of the Great Khan, Genghis Khan. They are by nature, aristocratic, aloof, snobbish and prissy."

Mango shows great concern. She wants to understand this strange, but very wise cat who speaks of many things she has never heard of or seen before.

"Tell me Mr. Cat, are you lost? Or, do you know your way home?"

"Unlike dogs who often get lost, I'm never lost. Because cats, unless they are careless cats, make a mental map of where they came from, where they are going and how they got there.

They know all the major points of the compass, North, South, East and West, which they use to find their way. Do you have such a map?"

"No, Mr. Cat, I've never seen such a map and I would not recognize one even if I saw one. But, I'm a bit curious as to how you found my avocado tree?

"I was visiting my friend, Mr. Joe Alley Cat, who lives in the alley behind your house. It was Mr. Joe Alley who suggested your avocado tree as a nice place to find shade from the hot sun."

"I'm pleased Mr. Cat, that Mr. Alley helped you find my avocado tree. I like it too."

"Good, for here in the shade, we can speak of many wonderful things, small things and big things. Love being the greatest of the big things."

"I know about love Mr. Cat, because my family showers me with love and affection."

"How do you know they love you, my little friend, for they may do that for every animal they meet?"

"I know they love me with a very special love, because they give me a warm bed to sleep on, food to eat, and when things frighten me they hold me close and softly pet me. Then, at night, when I lay down to sleep they cover me with a warm blanket to ward off the cold."

"Ahh, that sounds quite nice my friend. Is there someone in your family who loves you the most?"

"Little Miss Lisa Jones loves me the most."

"How do you know that?"

"Every night before we go to sleep, Miss Lisa and I say our prayers together and when we do, she always asks the Lord to protect and look after me."

The Siamese cat smiles. "You are a very lucky dog, my friend. Few are as lucky as you are. But as nice as this conversation has been, I must go now. Stay safe, until we meet again."

That evening, snuggled in her warm bed, Mango thinks about the new friend she has made and can hardly wait to introduce Mr. Cat to Miss Lisa. Oh, what wonderful stories they will share, she thinks.

Before, she falls asleep, she says a little prayer for Lisa. "God bless my Miss Lisa and make her well. Please Lord, I also humbly ask you to protect my new friend, Mr. Cat, from all harm and keep him safe during the long, dark night."

Somewhere in the heavens, the Lord is listening and happily grants Mango's prayer.

The next morning, Mango can hear Mother Jones say in a soft voice to Mr. Jones, "Thank God, our little girl's fever is gone."

Overjoyed that her sweet little master is getting better, Mango runs to the window, where she can see Mr. Cat wearing a big smile, patiently waiting for her under the branches of the big avocado tree.

ACTIVITY CENTER

FUN TIME

I CAN DO IT

YES, I CAN

NAME ME

Name 7 different breeds of dogs.

1. _____

2. _____

3. _____

4. _____

5. _____

6. _____

7. _____

PLEASE COLOR MR. CAT.

PLEASE GIVE A FRIENDLY CAT A FACE.

Cut out a photo of a
Siamese Cat
and paste it here.

**Take a photo of a
Friendly Dog
and paste it here.**

PLEASE COLOR ME

NEW WORDS

When you find a new word in the story, write it here.

1. ....

2. ....

3. ....

4. ....

5. ....

"FAMILY MEMBERS"

Please list all the members in the Cat family you can think of here, starting with their King, the Lion.

- ....

- ....

- ....

- ....

- ....

The Wonder of a Child's Memory Bank

Extensive research shows that the information present in the stories you read to your child at an early age, registers in their conscious and sub-conscious thinking for the rest of their life.

I encourage the parent reading Mango or any other story to their children, to discuss the story with them.

Ask them for positive feedback, and what they like about the story.

Ask them about the characters in the story and what they think the characters are saying to them.

Then ask yourself what you think those same characters are saying to you. You will be amazed at the results.

When the opportunity arises, compare your thoughts with those of your child. To foster meaningful interaction discuss the similarities and differences.

Ratna M. Dupont

www.ingramcontent.com/pod-product-compliance
Lightning Source LLC
Chambersburg PA
CBHW041542040426
42446CB00002B/196